by Rodney Martin

Contents

Introduction

This book shows you scenes from four different parts of the world (see map on back cover). Each scene has been photographed during different seasons. You can compare the photographs and see some of the ways plants and weather change with the seasons.

In any place, the seasons can be different from year to year. The photographs in this book show what happened during one year.

Seasons in cool, temperate climates

Some places in the world have warm summers an

In winter:
- deciduous trees lose their leaves;
- snow often covers the ground;
- the sky is dull.

In spring:
- snow melts;
- new buds appear on deciduous trees;
- crops begin to grow.

old winters. These places have four main seasons.

In summer:
- leaves grow on deciduous trees;
- crops grow and turn yellow;
- the sky is bright.

In autumn (fall):
- leaves on deciduous trees change colour then fall off;
- crops are harvested;
- the sky is dull.

5

Seasons in warm, temperate climates

Some places in the world have hot summers an

In winter:
- deciduous trees have no leaves;
- grasses grow;
- the sunshine is dull through clouds.

In spring:
- new leaf buds appear on deciduous trees;
- blossom grows on fruit trees;
- grasses grow thicker and taller.

In summer:
- leaves are fully grown on deciduous trees;
- fruit ripens and grasses die and turn yellow;
- the sunshine is bright and hot.

In autumn (fall):
- leaves on deciduous trees change colour then fall off;
- new grass shoots appear;
- the sky becomes more cloudy.

7

Seasons in polar climates

Places near the North and South Poles are alway
cool summers.

In winter: • snow covers everything;
                   • the sun cannot be seen at any time.

In spring: • snow still covers the ground;
                   • the days become longer.

ld. These places have long, cold winters and short,

In summer:
- leaves grow on deciduous trees;
- grasses grow;
- the sun shines all day and all night.

In autumn (fall):
- leaves on deciduous trees change colour then fall off;
- grasses die;
- the days become shorter.

Seasons in tropical climates

Places near the equator are always hot. These place

In the dry season:
- not much rain falls;
- ground is dry;
- grasses die;
- the sunshine is bright.

Place:	Jabiru, Australia
Date:	July
Temperature:	Av. max. 88°F/31°C
Sky:	Clear, sunny
Trees:	Green
Ground:	Dry; grasses dead

ve two main seasons each year — wet and dry.

In the wet season:
- rain falls nearly every day;
- ground is very wet;
- grasses grow tall and green;
- the sky is often cloudy.

Place:	Jabiru, Australia
Date:	January
Temperature:	Av. max. 91°F/33°C
Sky:	Cloudy
Trees:	Green
Ground:	Wet; grasses green

Winter in different places

Place: Abisko, Sweden
Date: January
Temperature: Av. max. 19°F/-7°C
Sky: No sunlight; moonlight only
Trees: Covered in ice
Ground: Frozen; snow covered

Place: Maidstone, England
Date: January
Temperature: Av. max. 43°F/6°C
Sky: Dull, overcast
Trees: Bare
Ground: Frozen; often snow covered

Place: Adelaide, Australia
Date: July
Temperature: Av. max. 59°F/15°C
Sky: Overcast
Trees: Some bare; some green
Ground: Damp; grasses green

Spring in different places

Place: Abisko, Sweden
Date: April
Temperature: Av. max. 30°F/-1° C
Sky: Dark; short days
Trees: Beginning to bud
Ground: Snow beginning to melt

Place: Maidstone, England
Date: April
Temperature: Av. max. 55°F/13°C
Sky: Dull
Trees: Leaf buds shooting
Ground: Damp, grasses green

Place: Adelaide, Australia
Date: October
Temperature: Av. max. 72°F/22°C
Sky: Overcast
Trees: Some trees blossom; some green
Ground: Damp; grasses green

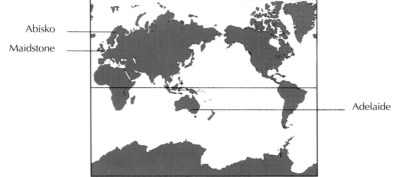

Abisko

Maidstone

Adelaide

13

Summer in different places

Place: Abisko, Sweden
Date: July
Temperature: Av. max. 59°F/15°C
Sky: Sun shines all day
& night
Trees: Leaves green
Ground: Grasses green

Place: Maidstone, England
Date: July
Temperature: Av. max. 72°F/22°C
Sky: Sunny
Trees: Leaves green
Ground: Grasses dry

Place: Adelaide, Australia
Date: January
Temperature: Av. max. 84°F/29°C
Sky: Sunny
Trees: Leaves green;
fruit ripe
Ground: Grasses dry

Autumn (fall) in different places

Place:	Abisko, Sweden
Date:	October
Temperature:	Av. max. 34°F/1°C
Sky:	Some clouds; short days
Trees:	Leaves brown & yellow
Ground:	Damp; grasses dying

Place:	Maidstone, England
Date:	October
Temperature:	Av. max. 57°F/14°C
Sky:	Cloudy
Trees:	Leaves brown
Ground:	Damp

Place:	Adelaide, Australia
Date:	April
Temperature:	Av. max. 72°F/22°C
Sky:	Overcast
Trees:	Some leaves red & gold; some green
Ground:	Damp; grasses green

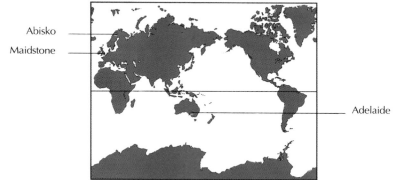

Abisko

Maidstone

Adelaide

15

A fruit tree in different seasons

In winter:
- branches are bare;
- tree is dormant;
- weather is cold.

In spring:
- leaf buds appear;
- blossom appears;
- weather is warm.

In summer:
- leaves have grown;
- fruit ripens;
- weather is hot.

In autumn (fall):
- leaves die and fall;
- fruit is picked or falls;
- weather is cool.